974.9

CHO

Choroszewski, Walter

The New Jersey We Love !

G

# The NEW JERSEY

## We Love!

## WALTER CHOROSZEWSKI

# The NEW JERSEY *We Love!*

First Printing 2009
Printed in Korea

ISBN: 1-932803-47-5
Library of Congress Control Number: 2009908775

## AESTHETIC PRESS, INC.

P.O. Box 5306, North Branch, NJ 08876-1303

Website: www.aestheticpress.com
Email: info@aestheticpress.com
Telephone: (908) 369-3777

# The New Jersey
## We Love!

WALTER CHOROSZEWSKI

Published by

AESTHETIC PRESS, INC.

New Jersey

*Dedicated to the loving memory of*
Joseph P. Hvizda
*"Uncle Joe"*

*Henry Hudson, sailing for the Dutch East India Company, anchored his ship the **Halve Maen** in Sandy Hook Bay on September 3, 1609. Although he is credited with its discovery 400 years ago, New Jersey was already home to the native Lenape people for thousands of years before the first European ships arrived in North America—almost a century before Hudson's arrival.*

*Giovanni da Verrazano and Estevan Gomez were possible visitors to New Jersey in the early 1500s. Some people have theorized that 500 years earlier, Vikings may have ventured much farther south than Newfoundland, perhaps to the Jersey shore. I prefer to give credit to ALL the discoverers who have come before us. Thank you for this land called "New Jersey." It's not perfect, but there is plenty to love.*

I first fell in love with New Jersey as a child. I was born and raised in the coal region of northeastern Pennsylvania. During the recession of the 1950s some family members moved to New Jersey to seek employment in the state's burgeoning industrial complex. Summer visits to these relatives sometimes included a side trip to the Jersey Shore.

After the Korean War, my Uncle Joe moved to Newark, and he eventually settled in Elizabeth, where he worked as a machinist in local factories. As a young man he enjoyed weekend trips down the Shore and recalled a chance meeting with Frank Sinatra at a lounge in Atlantic City. Sinatra was doing some undercover market research when he sat next to my uncle at the bar and asked him what he thought of the new singer. My uncle replied that he thought he was *"Okay"*—not realizing it was Frank Sinatra, himself, until seeing his show later that evening.

It was my Uncle Joe who started a tradition of a summer vacation to Wildwood. Each year he would take me to a different neon-emblazoned motel where I learned to swim in the turquoise swimming pools, where I first experienced the salty waves of the ocean and where I first ate at a New Jersey diner and ordered the very exotic "veal parmigiana."

We drove to the Shore in Uncle Joe's high-finned Plymouth on cement superhighways that were unlike any roads in rural Pennsylvania. We would often stop for lunch at **Hot**

**Dog Johnny's** or stop for a frozen custard at a roadside stand.  We always brought home the boardwalk prizes, salt water taffy and sea shells as souvenirs.  On the drive back to Pennsylvania, we would be sure to stop at a South Jersey farm stand for some fresh sweet corn and Jersey tomatoes to share and enjoy at home.

Childhood vacations eventually waned and New Jersey temporarily faded from my life during college years at Penn State.  After graduation, I moved to New York City where I began a career as a photographer.  It wasn't until I returned to New Jersey in 1980 on assignment for my first book, **NEW JERSEY,** *A Scenic Discovery,* that I rediscovered the state.  Revisiting familiar locations brought back warm memories, and my photographic sojourns revealed new wonders and charm.

Although we have all heard the stereotypes, clichés and negatives (*some true —most are false*), we still cherish New Jersey's positive aspects which keep us here.  I believe I speak for many New Jerseyans in expressing a sincere love for our state.

We love New Jersey's unique geology and geography with its four physiographic provinces neatly packaged into a peninsula between two great rivers.  The distance from High Point to the Atlantic Coast is only a few hours drive.  Our volcanic past is apparent in the majestic diabase Palisades and the basaltic Watchung Ridges.  We love our mild temperate climate with four distinct seasons giving us floral springs, hot summers, crisp colorful autumns and an occasional snowfall in winter.

We love our state's rich history from the earliest Dutch, Swedish and English settlements  to New Jersey's pivotal role as the Crossroads of the American Revolution. Revolutionary sites are plentiful throughout our state. Morristown served as the military capital of the Revolution.  The initial retreat across New Jersey from the Hudson to the Delaware rivers was followed by triumphant victories at Trenton and Princeton.  The Revolution continued with winter encampments at Middlebrook and Morristown, as well as numerous skirmishes and battles, culminating in 1780 with the Battle of Monmouth.  A victorious General Washington gave his farewell orders at Rockingham, and both Princeton and Trenton each briefly served as the nation's capital in 1783 and 1784 respectively, during the time of  the Articles of Confederation.

New Jersey was also a cradle of the American Industrial Revolution which began in Paterson in the late 18th century.  The magnificent Great Falls of the Passaic River was the source of power for this revolution, and was recently recognized as a National Historical

Park. New Jersey continued to be at the vanguard of invention and technology well into the 20th century. Some of Thomas Alva Edison's finest ideas and inventions were created at Menlo Park and West Orange, New Jersey.

We are all aware that New Jersey is the most densely populated state in America, situated near the center of the Northeast Megalopolis in the shadows of New York and Philadelphia. We love the convenience of being so close to these major cities but we also enjoy New Jersey's own smaller cities with all the modern amenities they have to offer. Newark, Jersey City, Trenton, Camden and Atlantic City have museums, sporting venues, art galleries and theaters which provide us with culture and entertainment. Their urban eateries entice us to try a variety of international cuisines.

In addition to our cities we also love our suburban small towns and hamlets. We shop in neighborhood stores on Main Street, dine at the outside cafés or Jersey diners, and attend patriotic parades and band concerts in the parks. New Jersey also has a rural character with abundant open space, parks and preserves, where we can kayak the rivers or bike its country roads and trails.

New Jersey is still the "Garden State" with over ten thousand farms utilizing almost five million acres of finest farmland. We love attending the county 4-H fairs and festivals and getting "Jersey Fresh" fruits and vegetables from local pick-your-own farms or green markets.

Whether we are long-time New Jersey natives who can trace our ancestry to New Netherlands or we are transplants from another state across America; whether we are the children or grandchildren of Ellis Island immigrants or we are recent arrivals from all corners of the globe, we all call this melting pot "home." This is the New Jersey we love!

## ABOUT THE PHOTOGRAPHER

*Walter Choroszewski has been presenting a positive image of New Jersey for thirty years through his photographic creativity. He has published numerous wall calendars and coffee-table books about the state.*

*Walter's New Jersey photographs were used to launch the popular "New Jersey & You ...Perfect Together" state tourism campaign of the 1980s and 1990s. His images of the state have been featured in advertising promotions, corporate annual reports, on telephone directory covers and magazine covers, and his fine art prints of New Jersey are found in many public and private collections throughout the state.*

*Choroszewski is also a graphic designer, videographer and lecturer, speaking to school children and various adult groups, encouraging pride in New Jersey.*

*Walter and his wife, Susan, live in Somerset County.*

*The Palisades Sill, Palisades Interstate Park, Englewood*

*Paterson Great Falls National*
*Historical Park, Paterson* ▶

*Museum of Early Trades & Crafts, James Library Building (1900), Madison*

*Grover Cleveland Birthplace (1832), Caldwell*

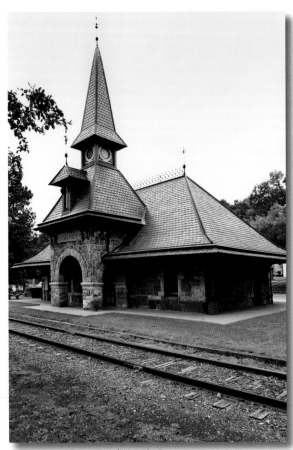

*Demarest Station (1872), Demarest*

*Frank R. Lautenberg*
*Secaucus Junction Station (2003), Secaucus*

*Fanwood Station (1874), Fanwood*

*Hoboken Terminal (1907), Hoboken* ▸

*Vincent R. Casciano Memorial Bridge and Newark Bay Railway Bridge, view from Bayonne*

*Cranberries at Golden Nugget Green Market, near Lambertville* ▶

*Strolling through Rudolph W. van der Goot Rose Garden at Colonial Park, Franklin Township*

*Summer annuals at the Donald B. Lacey Display Garden, Rutgers Gardens, New Brunswick*

17

*Hilltop Presbyterian Church of Mendham (1860)*

*Full moon rise over Round Valley Reservoir, Clinton Township* ▶

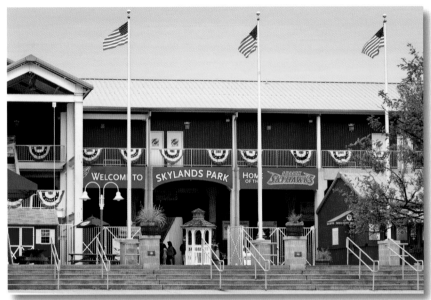

*Sussex Skyhawks, Skylands Park, Augusta*

*Trenton Thunder, Mercer County Waterfront Park, Trenton*

*New Jersey Jackals, Yogi Berra Stadium, Upper Montclair*

*Camden Riversharks, Campbell's Field Baseball Park, Camden*

*Somerset Patriots, TD Bank Ballpark, Bridgewater* ▶

*Ralston General Store Museum (1785), Mendham Township*

*Easton Tower (1899),*
*Paramus*

*Independence Day celebration at Morristown National Historical Park, Morristown*

*Patriot's Farewell Fountain, The Morristown Green, Morristown* ▸

*Houses border the Shrewsbury River, Rumson*

*The Twin Lights of Navesink (1862) crowns the Highlands* ▸

*Belmar*

*Holgate*

*Point Pleasant Beach*

*Sandy Hook*

*Brant Beach*

*Ocean City*

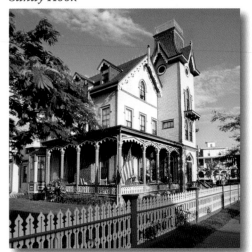

*Cape May*

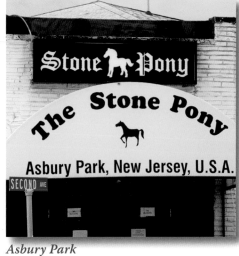

*Asbury Park*

*Ship Bottom*

*Casino skyline, Atlantic City*

*Pitman Grove Auditorium (1871), Pitman*

*The New Jersey State Capitol Complex, Trenton* ▶

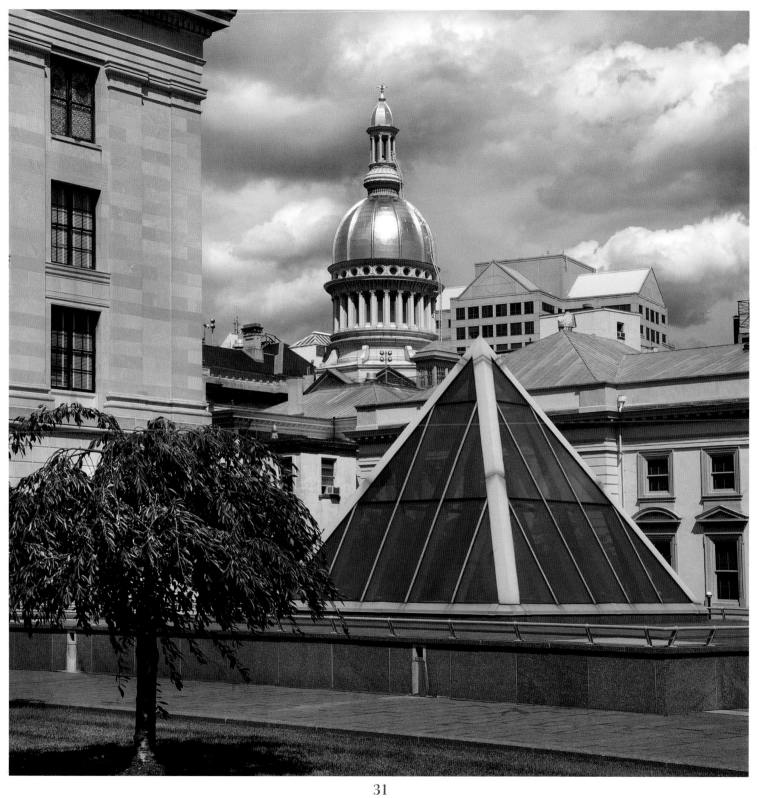

*Marble female figure, part of The Memoria Project,*
*a tribute to the victims of September 11th,*
*Veteran's Memorial Park, Highlands*

*"Lady Victory," New Jersey World War II Memorial, Trenton* ▶

32

*View of the Navesink River from Marine Park, Red Bank*

*The race begins! Tour of Somerville cycling series, Somerville*

*Lone cyclist at Scarborough Bridge (1959), Cherry Hill* ▶

*Misty morning,*
*Raven Rock,*
*Delaware Township*

*Sculling on*
*Carnegie Lake,*
*Princeton* ▶

*Over 400 years old, historic Salem Oak stands in the Friends Burial Ground, Salem*

*Westfield Community Band performs a summer concert at Mindowaskin Park, Westfield*

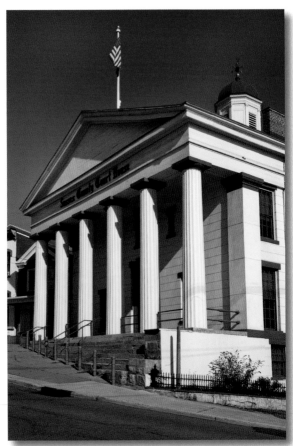

*Sussex County Courthouse (1847), Newton*

*Union County Courthouse (1903), Elizabeth*

*Somerset County Courthouse (1909), Somerville*

*Essex County Historic Courthouse (1907), Newark* ▶

*Lower Trenton Bridge (1928), Trenton*

*George Washington Bridge (1931), Fort Lee* ▸

*Flag raising on*
*Ocean Avenue Bridge*
*over Shark River,*
*Avon-by-the-Sea*

*Congress Hall Hotel (1816), Cape May*

QUEEN MARY

*Exploring the
Manasquan River,
Point Pleasant Beach*

*Kayaking on the
Delaware River,
Scudders Falls* ▸

*Tick Tock Diner, Clifton*

*Silver Coin Diner, Hammonton*

*The New Berlin Diner, Berlin*

*Americana Diner, East Windsor*

*Summit Diner, Summit*

Centennial Fountain, Bradley Beach

Fountain at War Memorial Park, Mays Landing ▸

*Colorful glass display at the Arthur Gorham Paperweight Shop, Wheaton Arts, Millville*

*Antiques shop window, Lambertville*

*Port Newark-Elizabeth Marine Terminal, Elizabeth*

*New Jersey State Fair, Sussex County Farm & Horse Show, Augusta* ▸

*Washington Township*

*Bedminster*

*Tewksbury*

*White Township*

*Park Ridge*

*Mansfield*

*Southampton*

*Peapack-Gladstone*

*Wantage*

*Farmscape along Rosemont-Ringoes Road, Delaware Township*

*Fishing at Monksville Reservoir, Long Pond Ironworks State Park, Ringwood*

*Merrill Creek Reservoir, Harmony Township* ▶

*Teetertown Ravine Natural Preserve, Lebanon Township*

*Tillman Ravine,*
*Stokes State Forest,*
*Sandyston Township*

*Eastern Bluebird, Sparta Wildlife Management Area, Sparta*

◀ *Virginia Bluebells, Duke Island Park, Bridgewater*

*Fresh snowfall blankets Brendan T. Byrne State Forest* ▶▶

*Rutgers Scarlet Knights play at Rutgers Stadium, Piscataway*

*The Paulsboro Oilers play beneath the Tinicum Rear Range Light, Paulsboro* ▸

*Autumn colors mirrored in the Musconetcong River, Saxton Falls*

*Sunset at Edwin B. Forsythe National Wildlife Refuge, Oceanville* ▸

*Cherry blossoms frame the Cathedral Basilica of the Sacred Heart (1899-1954), Newark*

*Sunlit snow at Delaware & Raritan Canal State Park, Griggstown*

*Little Red Schoolhouse (1866), Florham Park*

*Clara Barton School (1852), Bordentown*

*Goshen Public School (1872), Goshen*

*The Brick Academy (1809), Basking Ridge ▸*

*Mural, Camden County Althea R. Wright Administration Building, Camden*

*G. W. Helme Snuff Mill (1883), Helmetta* ▸

*Swamp milkweed at Johnsonburg Swamp Preserve, Frelinghuysen Township*

*Making friends at the Cumberland County 4-H Fair, Millville*

*"Lefrak Lighthouse" at the Newport waterfront, Jersey City*

*The "Evening Tide" plies the Kill Van Kull beneath the Bayonne Bridge* ▸

*Makepeace Lake Wildlife Management Area, Mullica Township*

*Apshawa Preserve, West Milford*

*Long Bridge Park, Hainesport*

*Colliers Mills Wildlife Management Area, Jackson Township*

*Aerial view of Sedge Islands Wildlife Management Area and Island Beach State Park, Berkeley Township*

*Quick Chek New Jersey Festival of Ballooning, Readington*

*Mural artist, Will Kasso, commissioned by the Trenton Downtown Association, Trenton* ▸

REACH THE
WORLD
BUT TOUCH
THE HOOD
FIRST!!!

.W.KASSO.

*Battleship New Jersey (BB62), the most decorated battleship in the United States Navy, is now a museum, Camden*

*78th Annual Independence Day Baby Parade, Lincoln Park, Rutherford* ▸

*Drumthwacket, official residence of the Governor of New Jersey, Princeton*

*Willowwood Arboretum, Chester Township*

*Greenwood Gardens, Short Hills*

*Van Vleck Gardens, Montclair*

*Hunterdon Arboretum, Clinton Township*

*Gardens at Drumthwacket, Princeton*

*Reeves-Reed Arboretum, Summit*

*Sayen Gardens, Hamilton*

*Smithville County Park, Eastampton*

*Brookdale Rose Garden, Bloomfield*

*Presby Memorial Iris Gardens, Upper Montclair*

*Green Sergeant's Bridge, Wickecheoke Creek, Delaware Township*

*Worthington State Forest, Hardwick Township* ▶

*Sunset, Maurice River, Brickboro*

*Sunrise, Atlantic City* ▶

*Catching a wave, Manasquan*

*Red Columbine at New Jersey State Botanical Gardens at Skylands, Ringwood*

*Somerset County Cultural Diversity Coalition's International*
*Festival, Raritan Valley Community College, Branchburg* ▸

*New Jersey Peach Festival, Mullica Hill*

*Corn Stop Farm Market, Route 206, Eastampton* ▶

*Oxford Furnace (1741),*
*Oxford*

*Swedish/Finnish log cabin (replica), Johan Printz Park, Salem*

*Cape May Lighthouse (1859), Cape May Point*

*Barnegat Lighthouse (1859), Barnegat Light*

*East Point Lighthouse (1849), Heislerville*

*Sandy Hook Lighthouse (1764), Gateway National Recreation Area, Sandy Hook* ▶

*Hadrosaurus foulkii,*
*sculpture by*
*John Giannotti,*
*Haddonfield*

*Sunrise illuminates*
*Great Swamp*
*National Wildlife Refuge* ▶

*Red Mill Museum
reflected in the South
Branch Raritan River,*
◄ *Clinton*

*Edison Memorial Tower,
Menlo Park,
Edison*

*Tripod Rock, Pyramid Mountain Natural Historical Area, Montville*

*Outcrop of Shawangunk Formation
at the summit of Kittatinny Mountain,
High Point State Park ▸*

*Acorn Hall (1853), Morristown*

*Holmes-Hendrickson House (1754), Holmdel*

*Crane-Phillips House (1840), Cranford*

*Isaac Van Campen House (1754), Walpack*

*Morven (1754), former home of Richard Stockton,*
*signer of the Declaration of Independence, Princeton*

*20th century Mail Pouch Tobacco advertising on Baker Theater (1880), Dover*

*Jam session at the Pickin' Shed, Albert Music Hall, Waretown* ▶

*Hot Dog Johnny's (1944), Buttzville*

◄ *Lucy the Elephant (1881), Margate*

*Boats line the lagoon near Barnegat Bay, Mantoloking*

*Tucker's Island Lighthouse (replica), the centerpiece of Tuckerton Seaport Museum, Tuckerton*

*Presbyterian Church (1745), Springfield*

*Boxwood Hall (1750s), Elizabeth*

*Washington Rock State Park, Green Brook*

*Fort Lee Historic Park, Fort Lee*

*Monmouth Battlefield S.P., Manalapan*

*Red Bank Battlefield Park, National Park*

*Hancock House (1734), Hancock's Bridge*

*Old Barracks Museum (1758), Trenton*

*Rockingham (1760s), Kingston*

*Wick House (1747-1750)*
*and Kitchen Garden,*
*Morristown National*
*Historical Park,*
*Morristown*

*Peregrine Falcon perched on Route 3 Bridge (West), Secaucus*

*View of Downtown Waterfront*
*skyline from Harborside south pier,*
*Exchange Place, Jersey City* ▶

*Eagle statue welcomes visitors to New Jersey State Botanical Gardens at Skylands, Ringwood*

*Morning ascension,*
*Quick Chek New Jersey*
*Festival of Ballooning,*
*Readington*

*Hereford Inlet Lighthouse (1874) towers above the dunes at Anglesea, North Wildwood*

*Mid-Atlantic Center For the Arts,*
*Emlen Physick Estate (1879),*
◀ *Cape May*

*Betsy Ross Bridge and Delair Bridge span the Delaware River, Pennsauken* ▶▶

*Pontoon boat eco-tour of Hackensack Meadowlands*